DEVELOP A WINNING STRATEGY
FOR YOUR MOST PROFITABLE YEAR EVER!

FINISH

IN THE
FAITH
LANE

4TH QUARTER PROFIT PLAYBOOK

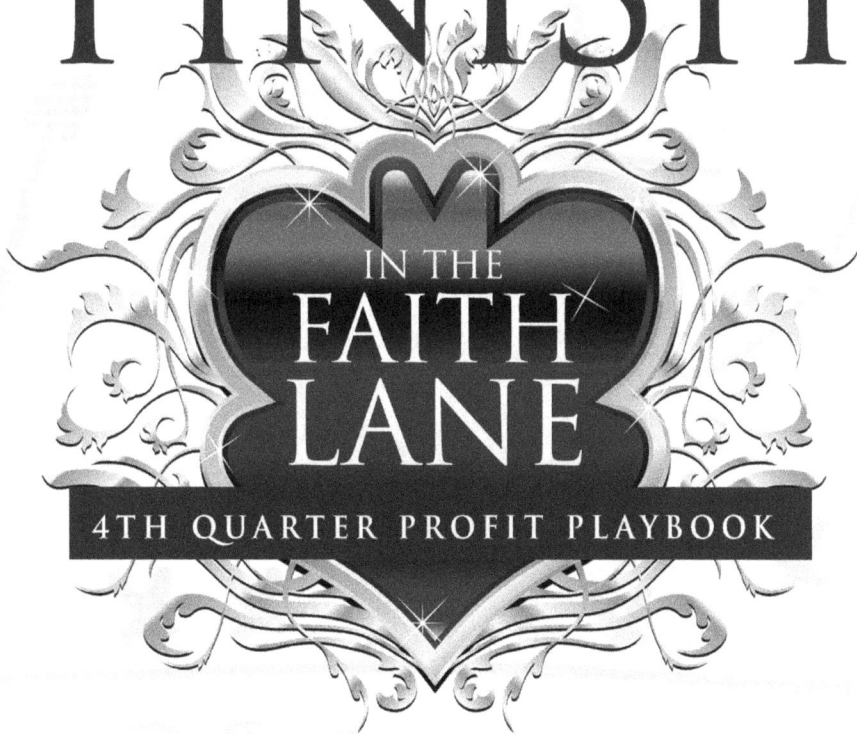

DANIELA GABRIELLE

ALSO BY DANIELA GABRIELLE

Fly Free: Finding the Courage to Live Without Limitations

Big Mouth Big Dreams: Your Guide To Speaking BIG Dreams Into Existence

Profit In The Faith Lane: Profitability Planner, Vol. I

Profit In The Faith Lane: Profitability Planner, Vol. II

My Life In The Faith Lane: Notebook, Vol. I

My Life In The Faith Lane: Notebook, Vol. II

motique media

www.danielaGabrielle.com | www.intheFaithLane.com

ISBN:0692570381
ISBN-13:9780692570388

DEDICATION

Finish In The Faith Lane is dedicated those crazy enough to complete their life mission while generating profitable revenue that has the power to create change in their own sphere of influence.

May this playbook unlock winning strategies that produce multiple streams of INCOME AND AFFLUENCE.

CONTENTS

FL Unlocking Your Profit Playbook

"It is usually those crazy enough to ignore the status quo and dare to do the unthinkable that achieve greatness. Be one of the crazy ones!"
-Daniela Gabrielle

INTRODUCTION

How you FINISH is predicated on how you start!

How many times have you gone into a new year with so much optimism only to find yourself so far from your initial vision by mid-year? Many times, it's not that you are incapable of achieving profitable and productive milestones, but that you have not been intentional in holding yourself accountable to a year-end vision.

Here's my story:

For years I would boldly declare, "I'm going to write my book this year!" Year in and year out, "I'm going to write my book this year!" and I'd get back to the end of the year with no manuscript, no cover, and most of all no book! I may get the outline together or even create a buzz, but I'd never finish the actual book.

I was constantly disappointing my audience and myself as this cycle continued year after year. Instead of building confidence in my dreams, I was constantly self-sabotaging my God-given assignment. The truth about my lack of finishing was that not only did it stifle my own progress, it was holding up someone who needed what I had.

One year I had this incredible epiphany! As a marketing manager for a corporation, I had been developing revenue plans that were yielding millions of dollars in year over year revenue growth. I was able to help operators reach their financial projections through practical and programmatic goals that were executed throughout the year, YET I was not experiencing year over year growth in my own personal finances and brand goals.

Why?

Because I was not investing the same time into planning to profit and being productive in the same way I was for those organizations. Then it clicked, if I were to build my own personal revenue plan and marketing plan, I too could see year over year growth.

I did just that! I got clear about my message for the year, developed my revenue channels, discovered what I needed to create into to launch those channels, mapped out a marketing plan and held myself accountable to implementing my plan. A three-year plan to transition into full-time entrepreneurship was shaved down to two years and with these yearly plans I was accomplishing more in a year than others completed in a lifetime.

It wasn't luck nor was it the alignment of any stars. It was my willingness to seek God about His BIG plan for my life, being crazy enough to believe his plans for my life and then having the wisdom to map out a practical plan to max out every gift that God had given me to experience profitable results!

Since then, I have experienced some of the most indescribable miracles in the marketplace. I have watched my clients soar into careers they only dreamed of, helped authors and speakers find and release their voice, and positioned myself for the next phase of my own BIG dream.

It all started by positioning my life in what I call the Faith Lane and being committed to finish everything God has charged me to do with Him year after year. When you connect God's purpose with your passion, you become unstoppable. There's NOTHING that you cannot do.

This is the perfect time to break the glass ceiling over your life and experience one of the most profitable…*and productive* years that you have experienced. It all starts with stepping into the Faith Lane. Are you willing to submit your life to his BIG plan and acknowledge that there is no success without God?

If you're ready say this small, but powerful prayer with me:

"Lord, I'm stepping into the Faith Lane!"

Now that you have tapped into the supernatural power of God that helps you to succeed in all that you do, it's time to FINISH IN THE FAITH LANE!

Let's talk...

We all have those areas in our lives where we become stuck and although we know that our next level depends on it, it seems like it's impossible to breakthrough unless we finish what we started.

Whether you are a high powered executive ready to elevate your career, a CEO wanting to take your company to the next level, or an entrepreneur looking to create streams of income for your family, the key to success is to have a plan that helps you finish what you started!

There is no success without completion. You have to determine in your heart that you will finish what needs to be completed so that you can push your vision forward and experience the growth that God has promised you!

This is your year to FINISH!

Finish what you set out for this year while learning how to build upon one fiscal year to grow successfully into the next one. The 4th quarter in any organization, brand or business is what I like to call the bridge season. It connects the successes and opportunities for growth of one season to the next season for year over year increase.

As you build your personalized 4th Quarter Playbook, I will walk you through four profit plays that will build upon one another to create a sustainable plan that's productive, profitable and practical.

Let's build your playbook!

Play of The Day

THE FINISHER'S
CREED

I possess the creative power to speak!

To speak into my purpose,

To speak my assignment into alignment,

To speak what I need for success into existence,

To speak what is not as it is

And to speak into the lives of those I am called to impact and influence.

I speak over my life that in everything I do,

I am a finisher!

I finish what I start,

I witness my ideas come to fruition,

And I experience explosive growth and profit because I finish!

I am a finisher!

Finishing is contagious.

When I finish, I inspire others to finish too.

We all win, because we all FINISH!

Finishing is my portion,

Completion is my inheritance,

Profit becomes my reward!

Profit 1 Play

MINDSET, MESSAGE & MOUNTAINS

"Every great revenue plan is built on a strong foundation."
-Daniela Gabrielle

A weak foundation yields unsteady results.

Every great revenue plan is built on a strong foundation. Before you can project for your most profitable year ever, you must create a platform in which that plan can stand on throughout the year. I would love to tell you that you'll build your profit playbook and that everything will go exactly as planned, but it won't. Life has unforeseen plot twists that we all experience, but the foundation is what allows our faith to stand strong and our hearts to remain open to navigating to our goal using the strategies set in our plans.

This is your foundation. You'll get to the heart of your vision, assignment, and purpose for this new fiscal year, allowing you to forecast a year that's not only profitable, but is surrounded by your values, purpose, and passion.

MINDSET

It All Starts In The Mind.

Your most profitable comeback ever starts with believing that you are worthy to build a profitable business or brand. Understanding that you are worthy of the lifestyle you see for yourself is vital in building your confidence to take action in your profitable lifestyle. My confidence in the statement, "Get ready for the most profitable comeback ever" is rooted in my faith. For me, it is my faith in God and it is his word, the Bible that I stand on. You need an anchor to stand on.

Identify three scriptures or faith-based statements that anchor your right and ability to profit:

1)

2)

3)

Play of The Day

MY WORTH STATMENT

I am worthy to experience my most profitable year ever because

_____,

_____

and _____

(insert your statements from the previous exercise).

Rebuild Your Thoughts.

To move forward, it's important to rebuild how you think about your business or professional brand. Your thoughts towards what you do will impact your ability to go BIG in your vision and present it BIG to the world. List ten powerfully positive thoughts to that have about your new fiscal year.

1) _____

2) _____

3) _____

4) _____

5) _____

6) _____

7) _____

8) _____

9) _____

10) _____

Getting To The Heart of Your Fiscal Year

If you're going to lead yourself or your organization to it's most profitable year ever, it's important that you know yourself as a leader and are clear on how you want to present that to the world. Understanding what your strengths and opportunities for growth are will help you identify the right way to strategize profitable growth.

For example, one of my greatest struggles has been the transition between being a solopreneur (running multiple companies as an army of one) to becoming a CEO leading a profitable business ventures with massive teams. Until I deal with what holds me back from making that transition, my profit margin will be limited because my actions are not aligned with my potential.

This is where you stretch out! Ditch the things that do not serve you in order to more effectively serve others. This is where you discover and become integral to your truth.

Your rise to greatness lies in honoring the gift of YOU!

Who am I as a high performing profitable professional?

_____

_____

_____

_____

Why do I want to be a high performing profitable professional?

_____

_____

_____

_____

Who do I want to serve? Why?

_____

_____

_____

_____

What do I stand for?

_____

_____

_____

_____

What four characteristics would I want people to identify me with as a high performing profitable professional?

1. _____
2. _____
3. _____
4. _____

What legacy do I want to leave?

_____

_____

_____

_____

Armed and Dangerous.

You are armed with everything you need to build a profitable fiscal year. All you need to do pull it out of you. It's time to recognize just how ready you are for your most profitable year ever!

What skills do I possess that will contribute to my most profitable year?

1) _____

2) _____

3) _____

4) _____

5) _____

6) _____

7) _____

8) _____

9) _____

10) _____

What skills am I lacking that I need for my most profitable year?

1) _____

2) _____

3) _____

4) _____

5) _____

6) _____

7) _____

8) _____

9) _____

10) _____

What do I feel will be my biggest challenges this fiscal year?

_____

_____

_____

_____

_____

_____

_____

_____

_____

_____

How can I work through those challenges?

_____

_____

_____

_____

_____

_____

_____

_____

_____

_____

_____

PRIORITY & PRODUCTIVITY CHART

Think through your new responsibilities as a profitable professional *(sales, marketing, business development, product development, customer service, managing employees, ect.)*. Identify your strengths, weaknesses and opportunities to delegate so that you can create a strategy to enjoy your most profitable year yet.

DO	DEVELOP
I'm Good At It & I Enjoy Doing It	I'm Not SO Good At It **but** I Enjoy Doing It

DELEGATE	DUMP
I'm Good At It **but** I Hate Doing It	I'm Not SO Good At It & I Hate Doing It

DO- these are the tasks you focus on this fiscal year

DEVELOP- these are the tasks you continue to develop with the assistance of a continuing education, professional development, coaching and/or mentorship

DELEGATE- these are the tasks that you delegate to a team member or intern with your leadership and guidance

DUMP- these are the task you outsource to a proven, established & trustworthy professional to handle so that you can focus on the things you thrive in

MESSAGE

This is where your fiscal year vision will be birthed. In order to win, you must first visualize the win. Then the pathway to it will appear. You fiscal year message is how you will interface with the world over the next twelve months. It is the pulse of your vision. How you move in the marketplace is all rooted in this message.

Imagine The Field.

Close your eyes and envision your new PROFTABLE fiscal year. What does it look like? What does it consist of? How are you positioned? Really allow yourself to become immersed in the visualization.

Now press in deeper. Ask the Lord to reveal his perfect plans for your year. What do you have to give the world in the New Year? What do you have to say, to teach, to impact, to lead us to going into a new year?

Ahhhhh… are you there yet? Can you see your brand emerging? Do you feel your gifts arising? Is your target audience there, receiving what you have to offer and paying you exactly what you're worth?

Feel that purpose-filled profit moving and flowing throughout your accounts. See your overflow creating a life where you are a conduit for wealth. You're creating jobs. Building lives. Transforming cities. Influencing nations.

Let your vision expand. Ask of the Lord again, "Please show me your perfect plan for this fiscal year." Now look! Look closely; your vision should be getting bigger and more fine-tuned. You should be reaching a place where he's showing you things that you never imagined you'd do.

That's it! He's talking to you. Those BIG super sized plans are downloading. Don't shut down, open your heart and receive. This is the download that you need.

MY NEW YEAR VISION

Use this space to record your vision. You can draw, write and post pictures based on what inspires and connects you with it the most.

IDENTIFY. What is your fiscal year message?

Now that you've had a glimpse of your new year, it's time to wrap that into messaging that's clear, concise and conducive to your vision and goals. This will allow you and you audience to maintain focus throughout the year on what you wanted to achieve.

This Year's Theme/Central Message
(i.e. 2016 <u>Your</u> Most Profitable Comeback Ever!)

Key Points	Key Words

Goals

GETTING TO THE CORE.

In our pursuit to accomplish or have success in business, we often rush past getting to the core of why we do things. The power of living a life in the Faith Lane is not only about financial success; it is about using our success for greater good. Your message should impact you just as much as it does other people. You should become the first fruit so to speak of your message.

You message impacting you and others lends credence to the service or products you are selling. You don't have to already have conquered the message, but it definitely should be influencing your life in an authentic way. Defining the core of your year will give you the strength to move forward, even when you experience shifts in the plan.

PROFIT PROFILE

I went into 2015 with the message, Get Ready For The Most Profitable Year Ever. My assignment was to equip those willing to align their lives with God's BIG plan on how to live authentically profitable lives in the Faith Lane. I sat down, wrote out the vision, put together the profit plan and then life happened. The derailing I felt I was experiencing devastated me. How was I supposed to experience the most profitable year ever facing homelessness, loosing a business and managing an undiagnosed debilitating health issue? How could I remain integral to the message that God released through me when it felt impossible?

I couldn't see a profitable outcome in any way, shape or form. At that point the idea of exceeding all my years financially seemed like fantasy. I would've given anything for *"just enough"* at that point.

All I saw was disappointment and despair. It was in that place to I often lost sight of the plan, refused to pull out my profit plays and for a season felt incapable of completing my assignment for the year. I disconnected from the core for a season, but even in my frustration I found myself drawing on God's promise and relinquishing my plans for his. I made some missteps along the way, but one day in a fit of disappointment God stopped me and took me back to these core principles I'm encouraging you to define.

It was in that place that I realized:

1) Homelessness hadn't stopped my impact.
2) Transition hadn't eroded my influence.
3) Illness couldn't stop my assignment.
4) Life could never interrupt God's promises.

The first half of the year had been pure turmoil, but God was able to show me how even though things hadn't gone according to plan, they had gone according to purpose. Even in rebuilding, he positioned me in my most profitable year ever and began charting my path to double that for next year. I learned through that experience, that God works well in recovery and that when we have a robust plan there's room for God to take you off script and still reach your goals.

Dig deep with God for an understanding of what they new year calls for and calls you to. This will be one of your most utilized profit plays.

IMPACT

How does God want your fiscal year message to impact *your* life?

_____

_____

_____

How does God want your fiscal year message to impact *the lives of others*?

_____

_____

_____

INFLUENCE

Describe the level of influence you believe that your fiscal year message will have.

_____

_____

_____

ASSIGNMENT

You understand your New Year vision; now define your assignment for the New Year.

_____

_____

_____

PROMISE

Every vision has a promise attached to it. Identify the promise for the New Year.

_____

_____

_____

MOUNTAINS

There are seven spheres of influence that impact society, these are commonly called the Seven Mountains of Influence. As leaders, we are called to be people of influence and agents of change. We have the ability to bring transformation to the world around us using our skills and passion.

Your most profitable year ever, should be rooted in your sphere of influence and the mountains that you are called to impact. This is a major part of merging into your Faith Lane.

When you get in your gift zone you are sure to score…REPEATEDLY!

IDENTIFY YOUR MOUNTAIN

Considering your message for the year, what mountains are you called to influence?

1) Arts and Entertainment 2) Business 3) Family 4) Government

5) Religion 6) Education 7) Media

Primary Mountain	Secondary Mountain	Supporting Mountain

For each area, explore why you believe you're called to each mountain.

For each area, explore how you are called to each mountain.

Overtime Plays
WINNING THOUGHTS • DREAMS • IDEAS • PLANS

Overtime Plays

WINNING THOUGHTS · DREAMS · IDEAS · PLANS

Profit 2 Play

MONETIZATION

module two is dedicated to Jack and Jennie

~Thank you for believing that there was more inside of me!~

"Don't love your job, it can't love you back"

-Jack Scott Niles

December 22, 1963 - February 8, 2010

Great ideas! Great messages! Great branding! They're all wonderful, but they have no impact without a result.

The fruit of your life should be profit.

I'll never forget arriving to my first day of work as a fresh new marketing coordinator. I remember is like it was yesterday. The director of the account says, "Oh, you'll make signs, blah, blah, blah…" Then in the deepest south Louisiana voice I had ever heard I hear, "Daniela, you are NOT a sign maker!" It was my new district manager, the BIG boss, Jack. I didn't know it at the time, but he was the one that would push me out of my comfort zone and challenge me to do things as marketing professional that always told myself I was not gifted for. I wasn't a numbers gal! I was a creative professional. Or at least that's what I thought until I met Jack… *and Jennie.*

It's amazing how we limit ourselves until we come in contact with someone who has the innate ability to stretch us to our new level of potential. That's what's happening now. Even as you're reading this story, God is stretching you. You may think you can't create a revenue plan. You might even be thinking, "I don't even have anything to sell," but hang in there. The monetization plan inside of you is about to leap like Elizabeth's baby did in her womb when she came in contact with Mary carrying baby Jesus. I'm telling you, *a "yes I can"* is about to rise up in you!

Okay, let's get back to the story…

Puzzled and confused as to what my job actually was. I found myself stuck between where I had been, which was marketing graphic designer and art director, and where I was called to be, a marketing professional that shifted organizations into the black year over year.

Jack had made his position on what I *wasn't* very clear, but I was missing the pathway to get there. If I'm not a sign maker, what am I? We talk and he tells me, "I've got you paired with the best marketing professional in the region. She'll teach you everything you need to know, if you'll listen. Watch her, follow her and take everything she can give you."

Jack lifted my lid and showed me that there was more in me, but it was his marketing counterpart that showed me the way. One of the most valuable lessons she ever taught me was this definition of marketing:

Marketing Drives PROFITABLE revenue!

She taught me that it was my job to see opportunities for growth, to always look for solutions the impact top line sales and ignites the bottom line profit. It's easy to make things pretty, but can you make them sell? Can you convert ideas to income? Can you create cultures that keep customers coming back for more? Can you drive profitable revenue?

Under her mentorship I learned how to do just that. Between Jennie and Jack I got an MBA in Revenue Development and Revenue Driving. Through them coaching and leading me I became that problem solving, solution seeking revenue driver I was called to be.

Guess what? You will too!

Building a monetization map is about seeing the possibilities that lie within the gifts and skills you have. It's identifying how your fiscal year message can solve your audience's problems. One of my favorite quotes from Dr. IV Hilliard says, "He who solves problems, gets paid!"

Don't shy away from getting paid! You need profit to influence the world around you. You can't scale your mountains of influence broke. It's going to take PROFITABLE revenue to create change. You're going to need to overflow, so let's map out a path that allows you to experience the most profitable year ever!

FAITH LANE

PROFIT PLAY

First things first! You must be intentional in having the most profitable year ever. This means that after your entire overhead is paid, there are finances left over. Those finances could be used to re-invest into the book, launch another project or saved for future opportunities. Before you start putting numbers to your ideas, get a realistic look at your overhead and determine what you need to bring in, to establish realistic service and product prices.

Forecast Your Monthly Expenses

(**Include:** *Website maintenance, e-mail, software subscriptions, coaching/ consulting fees, lawyer retainers, insurance, marketing, printing, monthly brand upkeep, and ect.*)

Expense	Monthly Cost	Notes
Total:		

Forecast Your Fixed Costs for FY_____

(One-time investment items that will help you to achieve your FY____ vision, i.e. new computer, branding photo shoot, trainings, ect.)

Expense	Cost	Notes
Total:		

Forecast Your Labor for FY _____			
Position	Hourly Rate	Hours/Week	Monthly Cost
		Total:	

Determine **YOUR** Hourly Rate

How much do you need to make personally each month to make the time investment sufficient in FY _____? _____

How much time can you effectively spend working each week? _____

Start The Equation.

1) Break down your fixed costs into a monthly rate

_____ (Total fixed cost) / 12= Monthly Fixed Cost Rate

2) Find your monthly bottom line

_____ (monthly take home) + _____(monthly expenses)
+ _____ (monthly fixed cost rate)+ _____ (monthly labor) =
_____ (monthly bottom line)

3) Factor in your profit margin

What percentage of profit do you want to reach this fiscal year? _____

_____ (bottom line)/ _____%=
_____ (profit)

_____ (monthly profit) + _____
(bottom line)= _____ (monthly revenue goal)

4) Discover your hourly rate.

_____ (monthly revenue goal)/ ____ hrs a month = _____ hourly rate

PROFIT
PROFILE

Edna needs to take home $5,000/month working 10 hours a week. She has $5,000 worth of labor, monthly expenses and fixed expenses. To meet her bottom line and make a 10% profit, her hourly rate is $275.

Now that she knows her rate, it's time to price her programs and services. Let's look at her speaking services.

As a speaker, Edna's offers two one-hour speaking services. Based on her goals, a one-hour custom speaking engagement (one hour to speak, eight hours to prepare customized content and one additional hour for incidentals) would cost $2,750 plus travel and a standard speaking engagement (using her fiscal year message with pre-developed content) would cost $1,650 (one hour to speak, four hours to prepare and one additional hour for incidentals) plus travel outside of a 60-mile radius.

Using her speaking services alone, four custom speaking engagements per month would achieve Edna's monthly revenue goal.

FAITH
LANE

P R O F I T
P L A Y

Once you have an idea of what it really takes to be profitable, it's time to create some profitable ideas that you can possibly implement into your message. Use the space provided to brainstorm what you can do with this year's theme and focus. Some ideas may not be directly correlated with the theme, but get them all out and then you can flush through them and find the ones that are best for this year.

My BIG Ideas for Profit
(Write down your ideas along with thoughts of how you would price them)

Signature Products and Services

You have tons of content inside of you or your business that can be converted into products and services. Based on your fiscal year message and profit ideas, you'll want to identify a signature line that monetizes your message. This can be in addition to other revenue streams, but will be your main offering.

Creating your signature line can feel somewhat overwhelming, but don't let it be. I like to use my infamous "Focus On Three" strategy to build this. Instead of offering a million and one options, build one three-tiered signature line.

TIER ONE

This is a product or service that serves more of the masses within your audience. It should be something that you can create once and provide multiple times. Your tier one product of service should be affordable and the lowest costing offering you provide. Information products commonly fall into tier one products or services.

Info Products

(Physical Resources)

Info products can be produced as either physical or virtual items. Products like books, audio series, albums, pre-loaded tablets with custom videos, links and other resources or t-shirt lines are all items that can be produced and then sold throughout the year.

(Direct Downloads)

Info products are audio series, video series, e-courses and etc. that can be downloaded by consumers from your website 24-7. This is passive income that, once created, doesn't require an additional time commitment.

There are two options for implementing this level:

OPTION 1: Create the product first and then using a marketing campaign to introduce it.

OPTION 2: Offer it as a free or reduced session to a select group and then roll the materials into an info product after the initial program is completed.

TIER TWO

This is your mid-level product or service that meets a more specific need and incorporates a higher value than the tier one product of service. Your tier two should cost more than the first, but less than the third. This is usually the tier that most people will buy into. One commonly used tier two approach is creating group services or products.

Group Services

Group services are programs that can be delivered to multiple people at one time. This can include seminars, conferences, group coaching, mastermind groups, membership programs and etc. The programs are time-bound and allow you to deliver content at an affordable price due to its mass audience. You can choose to implement these virtually or in person.

TIER THREE

Your third tier should be you! It should be highly customized with personalization and yield strong results. These are usually one-on-one or luxury products and services created for your high-end target audience.

PROFIT
PROFILE

Edna, the fashion guru and speaker's theme for the fiscal year is "Making Fashion Affordable." Her whole message is about creating a love for affordable fashion for men and women. She has an established platform and she's ready to profit in her Faith Lane. This would be an example of what her line would look like using her revenue goals.

Check Out Her Signature "Making Fashion Affordable" Line:

Tier One

Statement T-shirts $19

E-book with Audio Download $30

Tier Two

Video Membership Program $99/month

Red Carpet & Event Hosting $275/hour

Signature Speech $1,650/one-hour speech

Tier Three

    Customized Speeches $2,750/one-hour speech

    One-On-One Styling Sessions $275/hour plus fees

Using those basic products and services, she now has the foundation to create her revenue forecast for the entire year.

My Signature

PRODUCT & SERVICES LINE

Profit Is The Fruit of <u>YOUR</u> Life!

Product/ Service	Labor	Production	Price	Profit
Tier One				
Tier Two				
Tier Three				

Forecasting For The Future

Financial forecasting is a mixture of skill and adjustment. Having a clear understanding of what you need to make financially, in alignment with what you have to offer and a realistic number of people you are currently reaching are key to forecasting your most profitable year yet. Financial forecasting, in essence, is creating sales goals and then holding yourself accountable for meeting them.

The next step is actually mapping out your revenue plan for the year. This is where you determine your quarterly sales goals, break them into monthly milestones, and implement your plan to reach them.

Make It Easy!

1) Purchase and download DG's Revenue Plan template from our online bookstore at *www.intheFaithLane.com*

2) Once you finish your revenue plan, use Profit In The Faith Lane: Profitability Planner to manage your plan on a weekly, monthly and daily basis.

"Profitability is a shallow goal if it doesn't have a real purpose, and the purpose has to be share the profits with others."
-Howard Schultz

Overtime Plays

WINNING THOUGHTS · DREAMS · IDEAS · PLANS

Overtime Plays

WINNING THOUGHTS · DREAMS · IDEAS · PLANS

Profit 3 Play
MARKETING

"Our job is to connect to people, to interact with them in a way that leaves them better than we found them, more able to get where they'd like to go."
– Seth Godin

As a working professional, it is important that your marketing strategy is streamlined and easy to implement. Although there are many different marketing techniques, your PROFIT PLAY goal is to master three baseline marketing activities and commit to working them for the year. The more you use those methods, the better you'll get at them and, the easier marketing will become.

Don't overthink it!

Remember, marketing is driving profitable revenue. Your marketing activities should not only re-enforce your fiscal year message, but also create value and incite your target audience to invest in your products and services.

What should professionals DO to market themselves effectively?

➢ Build a community for their audience to gather

➢ Send out a regularly scheduled correspondence

➢ Schedule public and/or appearances on a regular basis

  o Show up where their target audience spends their time and have something worthwhile to offer them

  o Show value, meet needs and/or solve problems

Three Baseline Marketing Activities

➤ Create Community

➤ Build A List

➤ Display Your Value To Sell Your Services

Create Community

The key to driving profitable revenue is rooted in understanding *who* you serve, *how* you serve them, *what* they need and *where* they spend time and money. Knowing these four things help you to identify how to show up in the marketplace and from there you can begin to create your community.

It's important that you have a meeting place where those that are interested in what you offer can gather and really grow and experience your value. This can be a virtual community or an actual physical community. When choosing your community consider the following things:

Where does your target market spend more time, online or in person?

_____

What can your schedule handle?

_____

PROFIT
PROFILE

When I first started building my professional brand my first step was to create a virtual community where those that were interested in what my brand offered could all spend time together. At the time I was living in a small rural area that did not fit my target audience. My largest following was on the east coast, primarily in Atlanta, Georgia, USA.

How do I engage a market that doesn't dwell where I live?

Instead of excusing myself from building a BIG brand, I chose to start by creating a weekly community my Facebook page and free weekly conference calls. This is where I built my platform, on Monday Morning Push with Daniela Gabrielle. Throughout the week I would engage my audience through Facebook posts and then we would gather on the phone line every Monday morning at 8am EST where I would provide a complimentary motivational message and strategy for the week that aligned with my brand message.

The community I built through Monday Morning Push grew month after month and as I began to start releasing paid programs, this was where 70% of my clientele originated from. In addition to it being a place where potential consumers could experience my value, I was also able to convert the audio files into audio series that I sold online as automatic downloads.

Are your wheels turning yet? Can you see how I took this community and created multiple streams to revenue with it? This is something you want to consider when building your community.

Rule of Thumb:

Don't lock yourself into a community or community activity forever. Build a community that can grow and emerge with you. As you evolve, so will it. My recommendation is to commit to one platform for your community for the entire year.

When creating your community, approach it from the perspective of quality and not quantity. It's unproductive to have thousands of people in your private Facebook group or attending your month brunch event that are not engaged or interested in what you provide. Add a layer of exclusivity in your community and intentionally make environments that people what to be apart of.

Community Name _____

Community Platform _____

How Often Will You Engage In The Platform? _____

What Content Will You Contribute to the Platform?

[ ] Videos   [ ] Blog Posts   [ ] Branded Images

[ ] Written Tips   [ ] Articles   [ ] Podcasts

[ ] Conference Calls   [ ] Radio Broadcasts   [ ] _____

Build A List.

Building a strong e-mail list is where you begin to grow your brand and business. When someone joins your e-mail list, what they are saying is that they want what you have to offer.

It's important not only to build the list but also to build a relationship with those on your list. We will create a List Funnel to help you create PURPOSEFUL, POSITIVE & PROFITABLE relationships with your list.

THREE TIPS WITH ENGAGING WITH YOUR LIST:

Let them feel YOU.

Let your list get to know not just your company but who you are as the face of your brand. Be free to share with them some "not-so-sales" moments where they are able to connect with you as a real person. This will help them create quality connections with your brand.

Show them your VALUE.

Make it your business to pour valuable content into those who join your list. Give them a reason to share your content and to buy into what you have to offer. Don't be afraid to give them quality content. For every great piece of advice or strategy that you provide them, there's more where that came from.

Think of it the same way you would when investing in getting an ad or billboard. It takes content to sell content (just don't give away the whole farm).

Connect them to what you SELL.

Don't lose sight of the purpose of your list. It is to drive profitable revenue. When engaging with your list, provide them a connection to a product, service or resource that you sell or collect referral fees on. This can be done be simple links opposed to always sending out sales letters or ads. Remember your content to sales ratio should be 3 to 1. For every three content-based communications, there should be one sales-based communication.

My List Building Funnel

Choose You E-mail List Tool _____

Where will people go to join your list? _____

Connect the list to:

➢ Social Media Outlets

➢ E-mail Signatures

➢ Website

➢ Business Cards

What incentive will you give people for joining your e-mail list?

_____

_____

_____

How often will you communicate with your e-mail list?

_____

_____

_____

What content will you deliver?

[ ] Videos   [ ] Blog Posts   [ ] Branded Images

[ ] Written Tips   [ ] Articles   [ ] Podcasts

[ ] Conference Calls [ ] Radio Broadcasts   [ ] _____

Each communication will be connected to coincide with your monthly promotion calendar (page _____).

Display Your Value To Sell Your Services

The key to selling your products is creating a simple sales system with a call-to-action that is easily responded to. In order to sell your service, you must DISPLAY your value. Create a funnel to introduce what you offer to interested consumers; show them why they need what you offer, how it meets their needs and then give them a compelling call to action. In every layer of the funnel, your goal is to show your value.

Your Profit Play is to establish ONE system that you will use and perfect this year to sell all of your services, programs and products. This will streamline your marketing and sales efforts giving you time to focus on what you really love.

INTRODUCTION

How will you introduce products, programs and services in this year?

This should be done in a content-packed delivery method that provides stand-alone value. There is nothing that prospective clients hate more than feeling "sold." Your introduction platform, also known as an entryway activity, should be so strong that it would only be right to opt into the paid service or product. It should be THAT good!

[ ] Intro Video   [ ] Complimentary Call   [ ] Audio Download

[ ] Live Event   [ ] Free One-On-One Session   [ ] _____

OFFERING

How will you share the offering during the event?

_____

_____

_____

_____

_____

PROFIT PROFILE

Manuel is a financial services expert that is building his professional brand. He has a traditional corporate job, but also does speaking and consulting for additional revenue. Manuel is looking to launch a four-week finance course so he starts by creating a complimentary entryway finance workshop. When he gets there, Manuel gives his audience a solid content-filled session that leaves attendees fired up and ready for implementation.

He doesn't leave his audience there! At the end of the live event he shares how he can accelerate their results with his four-week finance course. Then he offers them a bonus for those ready to take immediate action.

Why didn't Manuel offer a discount?

Profitable revenue is generated by adding value instead of subtracting costs. When products and services are integrally priced you devalue your offerings by discounting them. Choose to add bonuses to your products or services to show value and create a demand for immediate action.

JUST SAY NO TO DISCOUNTS!

Think about it from a consumer's perspective, how many times have you opted to wait until the end of a season before buying something a full price because you knew that it would get marked down. Typically your thought becomes that if they can discount it than it wasn't worth what it was originally selling for in the first place. How often do you see luxury brands like Louis Vuitton, (high end car) or (high end jet) discounting their prices? You don't, because they set their prices based on their value and worth and are unapologetic about who can or cannot afford them.

Be unapologetic about your worth. You know what it costs to be who you are and bring what you bring to the marketplace.

CALL TO ACTION

How will consumers purchase your product/service?

[ ] Website [ ] Invoice

My Marketing Calendar

Month 1

Theme/Topic of the Month

Monthly Promotion (product or service)	

Monthly Community Activity

Monthly Media, Press or Public Appearance Activity

Monthly Sales Event or Activity

Call-To-Action	

Month 2

Theme/Topic of the Month

Monthly Promotion (product or service)	

Monthly Community Activity

Monthly Media, Press or Public Appearance Activity

Monthly Sales Event or Activity

Call-To-Action	

Month 3

Theme/Topic of the Month

Monthly Promotion (product or service)	

Monthly Community Activity

Monthly Media, Press or Public Appearance Activity

Monthly Sales Event or Activity

Call-To-Action	

Month 4

Theme/Topic of the Month

Monthly Promotion (product or service)	

Monthly Community Activity

Monthly Media, Press or Public Appearance Activity

Monthly Sales Event or Activity

Call-To-Action	

Month 5

Theme/Topic of the Month

Monthly Promotion (product or service)	

Monthly Community Activity

Monthly Media, Press or Public Appearance Activity

Monthly Sales Event or Activity

Call-To-Action	

Month 6

Theme/Topic of the Month

Monthly Promotion (product or service)	

Monthly Community Activity

Monthly Media, Press or Public Appearance Activity

Monthly Sales Event or Activity

Call-To-Action	

Month 7

Theme/Topic of the Month

Monthly Promotion (product or service)	

Monthly Community Activity

Monthly Media, Press or Public Appearance Activity

Monthly Sales Event or Activity

Call-To-Action	

Month 8

Theme/Topic of the Month

Monthly Promotion (product or service)	

Monthly Community Activity

Monthly Media, Press or Public Appearance Activity

Monthly Sales Event or Activity

Call-To-Action	

Month 9

Theme/Topic of the Month

Monthly Promotion (product or service)	

Monthly Community Activity

Monthly Media, Press or Public Appearance Activity

Monthly Sales Event or Activity

Call-To-Action	

Month 9

Theme/Topic of the Month

Monthly Promotion (product or service)	

Monthly Community Activity

Monthly Media, Press or Public Appearance Activity

Monthly Sales Event or Activity

Call-To-Action	

Month 10

Theme/Topic of the Month

Monthly Promotion (product or service)	

Monthly Community Activity

Monthly Media, Press or Public Appearance Activity

Monthly Sales Event or Activity

Call-To-Action	

Month 11

Theme/Topic of the Month

Monthly Promotion (product or service)	

Monthly Community Activity

Monthly Media, Press or Public Appearance Activity

Monthly Sales Event or Activity

Call-To-Action	

Month 12

Theme/Topic of the Month

Monthly Promotion (product or service)	

Monthly Community Activity

Monthly Media, Press or Public Appearance Activity

Monthly Sales Event or Activity

Call-To-Action	

Expanding Your Platform

As you are building your marketing plan, it's important that you plan for the growth of your platform. The great thing about building your signature product line and services is being able to take what you offer into places that it has never been before. This is your year to stretch out and invade spaces that you never imagined you would be able to invade.

This is not a year to think small. You owe it to the world to let your light into new places. Open your heart for a minute and take this in:

Your new year will bring you opportunities that you could only imagine. Platforms to share your expertise are opening for you. Choose to believe for the BIG things. Don't shrink back because of past experiences. Hope is rising now in your life. Believe again…build again…you are at the beginning of a brand new season in your life and career.

PROFIT PROFILE

Susan is a successful cosmetologist that has built a six-figure business doing hair. Now she is ready to expand her brand and take her gift to the masses. She begins to think over what she's passionate about and what she is skilled in and realizes that she has the tools to help new cosmetologists build their businesses with her Beauty Shop In A Box training kit.

Recommendation

The first obvious market for her would be to work with local cosmetology schools to have them either sell her kit or use them as textbooks in their program, but she goes deeper. To expand her platform, she researches the largest conferences and expos attended by cosmetologists and then she strategizes how she can get involved in one of those per year.

As someone that may not be known on a large enough platform, it may not be realistic that she can speak at the forum. What she can do is to purchase a booth and make that booth so interactive and memorable that it garners not only the attention of the attendees, but of the attending media and event organizers. It's not enough to have a product table, booths that get you noticed include a component that no one else is doing. She also needs to be sure to have branded gifts to provide to the organizer, keynote speakers and a few gifts that can be given away over the course of the event.

There are three strategic objectives of starting with a booth:

Industry Positioning

You are where your industry is

Tip: Don't be afraid to make the investment to have your brand at a high visibility event, but do have a plan to recover your investment through immediate action promotions. Be sure that your focus is solving a problem or meeting a need that particular audience.

Brand Recognition

You want your industry to recognize you or your business

Tip: Capture e-mail address or phone numbers and connect with attendees on social media on site so that the relationships can continue beyond the booth. She also needs to ensure that the messaging, art and feel of the booth mirror the online presence of her brand and business.

Platform Expansion

Build long-term professional relationships

Tip: Make room to meet beyond the booth. Set availability to invite 1-3 people that you may want to do business with or that could help you grow professionally to a one-on-one time with you. This could be for informational lunch, dinner or coffee, but remember that you want to use this time to get to know them professionally.

By now your faith should be rising and possibilities should be brewing in you. Begin to think about the spaces where your audience spends time and money in large numbers. How can you use those places to expand your platform?

Top Three Expansion Platforms

Platform 1:

Platform 2:

Platform 3:

Overtime Plays

WINNING THOUGHTS • DREAMS • IDEAS • PLANS

Overtime Plays

WINNING THOUGHTS · DREAMS · IDEAS · PLANS

Overtime Plays

WINNING THOUGHTS · DREAMS · IDEAS · PLANS

Profit 4 Play

MAPPING FOR MASSIVE MOMENTUM

"Every chapter ends with a period. Don't quit with an incomplete sentence."

-Daniela Gabrielle

What would you do if you had more time? What if you had more energy? What if you could really work the vision for your new fiscal year the way you wanted to? That's the power of the fourth quarter.

As a marketing professional, one of the most critical things I learned was to master the fourth quarter. If I could maximize the fourth quarter in three distinct ways I could relieve myself of some stress and actually manage the rest of the year versus spending my time creating, building, and responding to my market.

The first was to *finish strong*. Accounts ending with a strong profitable year-end move into the next fiscal year ahead of the game. If an account can end with a positive impact on its audience and have exceeded its financial goals, it automatically starts the New Year on a positive note.

Look at your year-end. How can you leave your mark on your audience and end this year with a bang? Consider a thank you event for loyal customers or something that will stimulate your revenue for year-end.

_____

_____

_____

_____

_____

_____

The second was to *create the plan and get ahead of the power curve.* Having an easy to implement and well thought out plan for the year is critical in having a year that navigates itself. For many, sitting down and going through the entirety of this book will feel like a lot, but I found that the years where I took the time to go through this process weren't just profitable, but they were much easier to manage. There was so much more room to explore and grow, because the year's foundation was solid.

The third was to *map it out.* I couldn't just have a plan, the plan needed to be synced to a calendar where I could give my teams and myself milestones, deadlines and realistic timelines to actually work the plan. This is how Profit In The Faith Lane: Profitability Planner was developed. I had to create a SYSTEM to manage our profitability. The system interweaved faith with practical tools to navigate towards profitability and gave me great success in the marketplace.

I strongly believe that there is not success without God.

I have tried over and over to separate my faith from my career, but the truth is that my faith is my greatest profit play. When I am stuck on a project or are not sure how to steer an account, it is in prayer and meditation that those strategies are released. I learned to look to heaven for assistance and it hasn't led me wrong yet.

People always say that you can't bring your religion to work and I agree, but you CAN bring God to work. You carry God in your heart and if you're willing, you can hear him guiding you in how to manage and lead your career or organization. The most liberating thing about faith is that it can be released in any atmosphere by listening and responding. This is how you will be able to lead your way to multiple steams of profitable revenue.

Profitable companies and professionals LEAD.

They lead their audience and their industry in a way that is impactful to the world around them. They're not responding to their markets, they are supplying them with what they need before they even need it. By the time you complete your first year utilizing and managing a fiscal year plan, you'll have fine-tuned your ability to lead in your organizations and industry.

Planning to lead your career or lead your company, gives you room to consistently elevate and enhance how you serve your target audience. You're able to come out of the creation lab and step into your industry where your success is bred and fed.

Now that you've discovered your New Year vision and developed your profit plan, it's time to spend the next 90-days maximizing the fourth quarter.

Declare this,

*"I am THE industry leader
and not just an industry provider!"*

Days 1-30: Wrap It.

Every Chapter Ends With A Period.

One of the most amazing things about being an author are the *ah-ha moments* discovered along the journey. As an author, I discovered that no matter what kind of book I wrote *every chapter ended with a period.*

We cannot enter into a new season of our lives, businesses, or careers without finalizing the season we are currently in. Before you become engulfed with what's in store for next year, a vital part of the transition is ending the year strong.

Look at last year's goals and plans. What is still lingering that needs to be completed? Write those items on the long lines to the left in the space below.

_____   _____

_____   _____

_____   _____

_____   _____

_____   _____

_____   _____

_____   _____

_____   _____

_____   _____

Now that you have identified what is unfinished, prioritize them into one of three categories and write their category to the right of them.

Wrap It – these are items that their completion is critical for finishing the current year strong and not completing them can impact the success of the next year. My recommendation is to limit your wrap it projects to no more than three high-impact, high importance projects that can be completed within the thirty-day period.

Roll It – These are items that flow with the vision of the New Year but are not critical to the completion of the year. Your intent is not to abandon them, but to roll them into next year's plan.

Shelf It- These items are good ideas, but *"not now"* ideas. For whatever reason this is not the right time to continue on with their efforts or to implement them so it makes sense to leave them on the shelf in case they become useful in the future. When you shelf something, it relieves you of the pressure of busy work. Busy work is unprofitable and robs you to energy to do the things that are most important in life. If you've struggled with busy work projects in the past, determine in your heart that moving forward you will say no to fruitless projects and busy work.

Once you have identified what you need to complete to wrap this fiscal year, use the first thirty days to finish those things. Assign yourself due dates for all of these projects in the space below and hold yourself accountable to finishing, If you finish prior to the thirty-day milestone, continue forward to the next phase immediately.

MY FINISH LIST

Project I   Due Date

_____   _____

Notes

_____
_____
_____
_____
_____
_____
_____
_____
_____
_____

Project II   Due Date

_____   _____

Notes

_____

_____

_____

_____

_____

_____

_____

Project III   Due Date

_____   _____

Notes

_____

_____

_____

_____

_____

_____

_____

_____

Declare this,

"I will finish what God has started in my life, career and business!"

Days 31-60: Create It.

Strong Programs Build Sustainable Growth.

You cannot serve your audience in creation mode. If you are constantly writing, working, putting stuff together, or developing something new, you never have an opportunity to execute your profit plan. It is vital that there are pockets of time set aside to create what you need to execute a strong service, product or program.

Your creation seasons should be in the downtimes of your year, times when you have automated revenue flowing or during times that are usually slow seasons. For example, a company that sells snow boots would not have a creation season between October and February. The best time for creation and product development would be spring giving them ample time to actually sell and promote their new line. Keep this in mind as you are mapping out your year.

Now that you've built your fiscal year profit plan, look back and identify what needs to be developed in order to execute that plan. Do you need a new website? Do you need to create workbooks or e-books for courses? Do you have videos to create? Are your marketing materials ready for the year? Have you scheduled out your special events and appearances?

What do you need create to your fiscal year? Write those items on the long lines to the left in the space below.

_____   _____

_____   _____

_____   _____

_____   _____

_____   _____

_____   _____

_____   _____

_____   _____

_____   _____

_____   _____

_____   _____

_____   _____

_____   _____

_____   _____

_____   _____

_____   _____

_____   _____

_____   _____

_____   _____

_____   _____

_____   _____

_____   _____

_____   _____

_____   _____

_____   _____

_____   _____

_____   _____

_____   _____

_____   _____

_____   _____

Now that you've identified what needs to be created for your New Year, begin to prioritize what needs to be done before the New Year and what needs to be done in other spaces of creation throughout New Year. Remember, creation times are typically down times, so be realistic in what should be done now and what can move into another creation season. Use the space to the right of each item to indicate NOW or enter the month that it will be developed.

You'll spend the next thirty days developing content, refreshing websites and creating what you need to launch your new fiscal year. Using your NOW list, prioritize how you can get those things completed over these next thirty days. Be careful not to over-complicate or overthink the process. The key to thriving in the creation season is to keep it simple.

PROFIT PROFILE

Ryan is a high-level corporate executive looking to expand is professional brand in the new year. As a part of his new vision he needed to create a website, publish a book and create his speaking materials for his launch, but as a husband, father and busy professional he was overwhelmed on how he could get through a thirty day development season.

What Ryan did was immediately schedule one three-day writing retreat at the beginning of the thirty days alone in a private location. He used those days to knock out manuscript for his book and turned it over to a company that would produce his book.

Upon his return, he agreed with his family to sacrificing two hours in the morning to work on the website content and the speaking content, then he would contract out projects to be designed and completed by professionals gifted in those areas. Mid-way in, Ryan also got the family involved in helping with photo shoots, video recordings and all of the fun stuff that he needed to finish his three projects. They worked on those things on Sundays as a part of their family time so that they weren't isolated during that period.

At the end of the thirty days the entire family celebrated with a special dinner where Ryan acknowledged the entire family's participation. It was an opportunity to stop and celebrate the completion of such a busy and sacrificial time.

Make Space To Create & The Celebrate.

Carve out ample time so that what you create isn't rushed. You may need to alter the time frame so that you launch your fiscal year with excellence. Use the space below to craft your plan *and* your celebration.

_____

_____

_____

_____

_____

_____

_____

_____

_____

_____

_____

_____

Declare this,

"I will not serve my audience in creation mode!"

Days 61-90: Bridge The Gap.

Have you heard the saying, "If it don't make money, it don't make sense"? There's such a level of truth in that. Your time and your gifts are valuable; don't waste your life on busy work. At this point you have finalized this year, you have your profit plan in hand. You are armed with everything you need to launch your most profitable year ever.

Now it's time to make the transition.

You've been knee-deep in your vision and it's in you. You can see it. You can feel it. Your excitement is overflowing! The next step is to impart your vision into the right people so that your excitement can be transferred to your industry.

Start with your team.

One of the biggest downfalls of organizations is communication. Managers often forget to download the vision to their staff. Whether you are a CEO or a freelance hairstylist, your team needs to see where you are going in your new year. They need to know and understand your message, goals, execution plan, and *their* personal gain.

Including what's in it for them allows them to connect with the vision in much more impactful way. It will help your team understand that it's not just all about you, but you recognize how the success of the whole affects the success of one.

Put together a presentation that presents your plan in a simplistic way and share it with them in an energizing and up beat environment. I usually hold a 4th quarter meeting with my teams and one with my family that includes music, a vision casting presentation, recognition of last year's accomplishments, and a revenue road map handout for the new year. I also give each attendee a planner, Profit In The Faith Lane (of course!), journal, My Life In The Faith Lane notebook (duh…) and a handpicked personal or professional development book. This session energizes the team and gets them fired up for the transition.

If you work solo or run your own company, I recommend that you include your family. They are a vital part of your success, they need to know and understand what you're working towards. This helps everyone get on the same page and begin moving in the same direction. I recommend that this is done as early in the fourth quarter as possible so that the team has time to let the vision settle in, ask questions, and have more in-depth training for the new year.

RELEASING MY VISION

My Fiscal Year		
Team Vision Release Meeting		
Team Members	Date	
	Location	
	Time	
	Duration	
	Order of Events	

Expand to your core.

Every professional has a core. This could be your core clients, loyal customers, or long-standing fans that support your endeavors financially. This is also where you want to draw in those that you would like to connect with and do business with on a high-level in the new year. Your core will be your greatest asset in the upcoming year. Having them understand your direction helps them understand how they can grow forward with you.

This session is not about your revenue goals; it's about your message and how you plan to use this message in the new year. You are imparting into them, the direction for where your company or career is going. At this session, I usually start with a look back on the year we came out of. This is where I allow the core to share how what I offer has impacted their lives or careers. Then I go into imparting the new message. This is usually your first run at delivering your signature message in the form of a keynote.

The goal of your core meeting is to inspire, empower, and provide special level of impartation privy only to this group. They should leave, not just understanding the vision, but with tools to move forward in that message. Like my team, I also sow into them by gifting attendees with a planner, journal and a bonus gift. I recommend that you have this session in the middle of the fourth quarter.

RELEASING MY VISION

My Fiscal Year		
VIP Vision Release Session		
Team Members	Date	
	Location	
	Time	
	Duration	
	Order of Events	

Launch your new year.

The final phase of shifting into your new fiscal year is getting your message out your target audience. Every day in the last thirty days of the fourth quarter you should be sharing and posting based on your message. I encourage you to use mixed media to do so *(i.e. videos, social media posts, quote images and blog entries)*. This will build excitement and get people curious about your message.

Think about short, but powerful, mixed media activities you will do in the thirty days leading up to the launch of your new year. Create a hash tag and name for this thirty-day campaign that builds excitement with your audience. The goal is to have them just as excited as you are about crossing over into a new season. Use this social media calendar to map those online activities.

Once you map out your social media plan, I recommend that you create your content and schedule these baseline postings for the thirty-day campaign.

Day One

8:00a Day Starter   _____

12:00noon Pick Me Up   _____

3:00pm Engagement   _____

6:00pm Engagement   _____

9:00pm Closer   _____

LIVE! Post (Choose the time)   _____

Day Two

8:00a Day Starter   _____

12:00noon Pick Me Up   _____

3:00pm Engagement   _____

6:00pm Engagement   _____

9:00pm Closer   _____

LIVE! Post (Choose the time)   _____

Day Three

8:00a Day Starter _____

12:00noon Pick Me Up _____

3:00pm Engagement _____

6:00pm Engagement _____

9:00pm Closer _____

LIVE! Post (Choose the time) _____

Day Four

8:00a Day Starter _____

12:00noon Pick Me Up _____

3:00pm Engagement _____

6:00pm Engagement _____

9:00pm Closer _____

LIVE! Post (Choose the time) _____

Day Five

8:00a Day Starter   _____

12:00noon Pick Me Up   _____

3:00pm Engagement   _____

6:00pm Engagement   _____

9:00pm Closer   _____

LIVE! Post (Choose the time)   _____

Day Six

8:00a Day Starter   _____

12:00noon Pick Me Up   _____

3:00pm Engagement   _____

6:00pm Engagement   _____

9:00pm Closer   _____

LIVE! Post (Choose the time)   _____

Day Seven

8:00a Day Starter _____

12:00noon Pick Me Up _____

3:00pm Engagement _____

6:00pm Engagement _____

9:00pm Closer _____

LIVE! Post (Choose the time) _____

Day Eight

8:00a Day Starter _____

12:00noon Pick Me Up _____

3:00pm Engagement _____

6:00pm Engagement _____

9:00pm Closer _____

LIVE! Post (Choose the time) _____

Day Nine

8:00a Day Starter   _____

12:00noon Pick Me Up   _____

3:00pm Engagement   _____

6:00pm Engagement   _____

9:00pm Closer   _____

  LIVE! Post (Choose the time)   _____

Day Ten

8:00a Day Starter   _____

12:00noon Pick Me Up   _____

3:00pm Engagement   _____

6:00pm Engagement   _____

9:00pm Closer   _____

LIVE! Post (Choose the time)   _____

Day Eleven

8:00a Day Starter   _____

12:00noon Pick Me Up   _____

3:00pm Engagement   _____

6:00pm Engagement   _____

9:00pm Closer   _____

LIVE! Post (Choose the time)   _____

Day Twelve

8:00a Day Starter   _____

12:00noon Pick Me Up   _____

3:00pm Engagement   _____

6:00pm Engagement   _____

9:00pm Closer   _____

LIVE! Post (Choose the time)   _____

Day Thirteen

8:00a Day Starter   _____

12:00noon Pick Me Up   _____

3:00pm Engagement   _____

6:00pm Engagement   _____

9:00pm Closer   _____

LIVE! Post (Choose the time) _____

Day Fourteen

8:00a Day Starter   _____

12:00noon Pick Me Up   _____

3:00pm Engagement   _____

6:00pm Engagement   _____

9:00pm Closer   _____

LIVE! Post (Choose the time) _____

Day Fifteen

8:00a Day Starter _____

12:00noon Pick Me Up _____

3:00pm Engagement _____

6:00pm Engagement _____

9:00pm Closer _____

LIVE! Post (Choose the time) _____

Day Sixteen

8:00a Day Starter _____

12:00noon Pick Me Up _____

3:00pm Engagement _____

6:00pm Engagement _____

9:00pm Closer _____

LIVE! Post (Choose the time) _____

Day Seventeen

8:00a Day Starter   _____

12:00noon Pick Me Up   _____

3:00pm Engagement   _____

6:00pm Engagement   _____

9:00pm Closer   _____

LIVE! Post (Choose the time) _____

Day Eighteen

8:00a Day Starter   _____

12:00noon Pick Me Up   _____

3:00pm Engagement   _____

6:00pm Engagement   _____

9:00pm Closer   _____

LIVE! Post (Choose the time) _____

Day Nineteen

8:00a Day Starter   _____

12:00noon Pick Me Up   _____

3:00pm Engagement   _____

6:00pm Engagement   _____

9:00pm Closer   _____

  LIVE! Post (Choose the time)   _____

Day Twenty

8:00a Day Starter   _____

12:00noon Pick Me Up   _____

3:00pm Engagement   _____

6:00pm Engagement   _____

9:00pm Closer   _____

LIVE! Post (Choose the time)   _____

Day Twenty-One

8:00a Day Starter   _____

12:00noon Pick Me Up   _____

3:00pm Engagement   _____

6:00pm Engagement   _____

9:00pm Closer   _____

LIVE! Post (Choose the time)   _____

Day Twenty-Two

8:00a Day Starter   _____

12:00noon Pick Me Up   _____

3:00pm Engagement   _____

6:00pm Engagement   _____

9:00pm Closer   _____

LIVE! Post (Choose the time)   _____

Day Twenty-Three

8:00a Day Starter _____

12:00noon Pick Me Up _____

3:00pm Engagement _____

6:00pm Engagement _____

9:00pm Closer _____

LIVE! Post (Choose the time) _____

Day Twenty-Four

8:00a Day Starter _____

12:00noon Pick Me Up _____

3:00pm Engagement _____

6:00pm Engagement _____

9:00pm Closer _____

LIVE! Post (Choose the time) _____

Day Twenty-Five

8:00a Day Starter   _____

12:00noon Pick Me Up   _____

3:00pm Engagement   _____

6:00pm Engagement   _____

9:00pm Closer   _____

LIVE! Post (Choose the time)   _____

Day Twenty-Six

8:00a Day Starter   _____

12:00noon Pick Me Up   _____

3:00pm Engagement   _____

6:00pm Engagement   _____

9:00pm Closer   _____

LIVE! Post (Choose the time)   _____

Day Twenty-Seven

8:00a Day Starter   _____

12:00noon Pick Me Up   _____

3:00pm Engagement   _____

6:00pm Engagement   _____

9:00pm Closer   _____

LIVE! Post (Choose the time)   _____

Day Twenty-Eight

8:00a Day Starter   _____

12:00noon Pick Me Up   _____

3:00pm Engagement   _____

6:00pm Engagement   _____

9:00pm Closer   _____

LIVE! Post (Choose the time)   _____

Day Twenty-Nine

8:00a Day Starter _____

12:00noon Pick Me Up _____

3:00pm Engagement _____

6:00pm Engagement _____

9:00pm Closer _____

LIVE! Post (Choose the time) _____

Day Thirty

8:00a Day Starter _____

12:00noon Pick Me Up _____

3:00pm Engagement _____

6:00pm Engagement _____

9:00pm Closer _____

LIVE! Post (Choose the time) _____

PROFIT
PROFILE

When I got the Life In The Faith Lane message, I launched an " I _____ in the Faith Lane" campaign where I had clients, friends, family and those willing to partner their platforms by allowing me to create a custom sharable photo with their photo and what they do in the Faith Lane. They would then post them and share them on their pages and I did the same thing. I used the hash tag #lifeintheFaithLane with the campaign. Since then the campaign has taken it's on form and now others are using the phrase to describe their lives.

That's the level of excitement that you want to create with your fiscal year message. Then you want to reach a pinnacle and explode your message into the hearts of your target audience with some type of complimentary launch event. Each year I host a Dream Development Summit via conference call where I team on the concepts and principles of my new year message. It is my first touch point with my audience.

I give them a high energy, high content, and high impact experience that is action oriented and helps them move into their year. As we discussed in our other modules, even complimentary events should lead to programs or products with monetary value so I usually use the platform to promote my January promotion and upcoming events.

You've shared with your team, imparted into your core, and now it's time to plan your launch. Take some time to create your launch event for the new year and get ready to kick-off your most profitable year ever! Make it fun, interactive, and reflective of your professional brand. It should have your brand written all over it.

LAUNCHING MY YEAR

My New Year Launch Event

Event Name _____

Theme _____

Location _____

Date(s) _____

Time(s) _____

Event Details

_____

_____

_____

Overtime Plays
WINNING THOUGHTS · DREAMS · IDEAS · PLANS

Overtime Plays

WINNING THOUGHTS • DREAMS • IDEAS • PLANS

Overtime Plays

WINNING THOUGHTS · DREAMS · IDEAS · PLANS

Declare this,

"I WILL launch my most profitable year ever!"

"God knows exactly what you need to thrive in this new year and if you are bold enough to trust him, he will lead you into places you've never dreamed of."

-Daniela Gabrielle

In sports, in life, and in business every playbook is different. No two playbooks will ever be the same, because it is YOUR secret handbook to learn faster, win more often, and finish with your desired level of growth. Don't compare profit plans with the next person, but instead trust that what you have built has been tailor-made by God for your success.

He knows YOU! God knows exactly what you need to thrive in this new year and if you are bold enough to trust him, he will lead you into places you've never dreamed of.

Here's the deal…

This profit playbook is the baseline to the experiences you are about to embark on. To maximize the journey, it's important that you learn to practice living your life in the Faith Lane. Learn to be in daily communication with God and allow him to navigate you through this thing called life. You'll find that this guide has focused you and that God will help you to hone in to where you need to be every step of the way.

The key to life in the Faith Lane is to listen and obey. When you get stuck, don't be afraid to take time outs to re-group and get direction from God. Often times we leave God out of the boardroom, out of the recording booth, out of the workplace in general, but taking God with you doesn't require you toting your Bible and quoting scriptures. It requires you giving him room to lead YOU. Trust me, as you let God give you strategies to lead your moves in business and the workplace, people will notice. They'll notice your disposition, they'll notice your success, but most of all they'll notice your resilience.

How many times will you hit a brick wall and continue to move forward? How many times will you fall and trust God to help you back up again? Finishing in the Faith Lane is as just as much about the valley experiences as it is about the mountaintop. One thing I love about professional football is that whether you play ten seconds or ten minutes you still get your contractual pay, because you were on the field.

As long as you show up to practice, do the groundwork and are prepared to move when the coach says go, you're going to get that check. It's the same way in life. Do the groundwork. Be prepared so that when God, your coach, puts you in the game you are ready to play. He rewards those who diligently seek him. Don't leave him out! Take him with you! Let his love and his power radiate from you to the darkest places in your industry. Now that's how you take God to work and watch your life PROFIT!

After the planning has been done.

Now here comes the hard part. Planning is easy, but it's what you do with your playbook day to day that will determine the amount of profitable growth that you experience. You are the CEO of your profit plan. You are the boss! You are the chief implementer! You are the head revenue manager in charge!

Will you take the plunge to not just finish in the Faith Lane, but to move the very existence of your life into the Faith Lane? Are you willing to do what you've never done to experience what you never had? Are you ready to give your life a deeper meaning?

It's game-time my friend! The only people who get paid are the people invested in the field. You've made your first investment, now it's time to activate the strategies to win!

Go. Do. Be.

"It's time to embrace your incredible profitable Life in the Faith Lane."

I love you to life,

Daniela Gabrielle

My Playbook Quick Reference Cheat Sheet

KEEP CALM AND PROFIT

FINISH

WWW.INTHEFAITHLANE.COM

DANIELA GABRIELLE
RELEASING YOU TO PURPOSE & THE MARKETPLACE

FAITH
LANE
AUTHOR &
FOUNDER

Daniela Gabrielle, The Transition Entrepreneur is a bestselling author and motivational speaker. As the CEO of MOTIQUE Dream Development Co., and its multiple subsidiaries, she has embraced the role of a serial entrepreneur, empowering others as a personal and professional development expert, business and branding consultant, and entertainment personality.

This media mogul chose to transform her life from ordinary to extraordinary by abandoning her comfortable surroundings to go after the life and career she always dreamed of. She has coined the phrase, "Live the Life You Love" and uses this mantra to help people across the globe change, transition and emerge.

For Booking Inquiries e-mail: info@danielaGabrielle.com

Corporate Training & Consulting
Seminars & Workshops
Red Carpet & Event Hosting
Keynote Speaking
Individual Training & Consulting

Stay Connected!

www.danielaGabrielle.com   **www.intheFaithLane.com**
www.facebook.com/chatDaniG   wwww.twitter.com/chatDaniD

www.ingramcontent.com/pod-product-compliance
Lightning Source LLC
Chambersburg PA
CBHW061818210326
41599CB00034B/7039